The National Poetry Series was established in 1978 to ensure the publication of five poetry books annually through five participating publishers. Publication is funded by the Lannan Foundation; Stephen Graham; Joyce & Seward Johnson Foundation; Juliet Lea Hillman Simonds; The Poetry Foundation; and, Olafur Olafsson.

2012 Competition Winners

the meatgirl whatever, by Kristin Hatch of San Francisco, CA
Chosen by K. Silem Mohammad, to be published by Fence Books

The Narrow Circle, by Nathan Hoks of Chicago, IL
Chosen by Dean Young, to be published by Penguin Books

The Cloud that Contained the Lightning, by Cynthia Lowen of Brooklyn, NY
Chosen by Nikky Finney, to be published by University of Georgia Press

Visiting Hours at the Color Line, by Ed Pavlić of Athens, GA
Chosen by Dan Beachy-Quick, to be published by Milkweed Editions

Failure and I Bury the Body, by Sasha West of Austin, TX
Chosen by D. Nurkse, to be published by HarperCollins Publishers

visiting hours at the color line

More by Ed Pavlić

But Here Are Small Clear Refractions

Winners Have Yet to Be Announced: A Song for Donny Hathaway

Labors Lost Left Unfinished

*Crossroads Modernism: Descent and Emergence in African American
Literary Culture*

Paraph of Bone & Other Kinds of Blue

VISITING HOURS AT THE COLOR LINE

poems

Ed Pavlić

milkweed
editions

Published 2013 by Milkweed Editions
Printed in the United States of America
Cover design by Jeenee Lee
Cover art © Henry Jackson, "Untitled #26-10"
Author photo by Sunčana Pavlić
13 14 15 16 17   5 4 3 2 1
First Edition

Milkweed Editions, an independent nonprofit publisher, gratefully acknowledges sustaining
support from the Bush Foundation; the Patrick and Aimee Butler Foundation; the Dougherty
Family Foundation; the Driscoll Foundation; the Jerome Foundation; the Lindquist & Vennum
Foundation; the McKnight Foundation; the voters of Minnesota through a Minnesota State Arts
Board Operating Support grant, thanks to a legislative appropriation from the arts and cultural
heritage fund; the National Endowment for the Arts; the Target Foundation; and other generous
contributions from foundations, corporations, and individuals. For a full listing of Milkweed
Editions supporters, please visit www.milkweed.org.

Library of Congress Cataloging-in-Publication Data

Pavlic, Edward M. (Edward Michael).
   [Poems. Selections]
   Visiting hours at the color line : poems / Ed Pavlic. -- First edition.
      pages cm
   Includes bibliographical references.
   ISBN 978-1-57131-460-4 (alk. paper)
   I. Title.
   PS3616.A9575V57 2013
   811'.6--dc23
                            2012051805

Milkweed Editions is committed to ecological stewardship. We strive to align our book
production practices with this principle, and to reduce the impact of our operations in the
environment. We are a member of the Green Press Initiative, a nonprofit coalition of publishers,
manufacturers, and authors working to protect the world's endangered forests and conserve
natural resources. *Visiting Hours at the Color Line* was printed on acid-free
30% postconsumer-waste paper by Versa Press, Inc.

For Stacey. For Adrienne, in continued presence. And, for Glo.

"There's always a 'more,' always a 'soon'."

Contents

I had to discover the demarcation line, if there was one. . . .
How to perceive, define, a line nearly too thin for the naked eye,
so mercurial, and so mighty.

—James Baldwin

To merely depict an action or a gesture is not my concern . . .
this tearing down of form, is a reminder to me of what we lose
of ourselves everyday—a reminder of the inevitable and the
battle to exist.

—Henry Jackson

You can't fake the feeling without feeling.

—Geraldine Hunt

visiting hours at the color line

Verbatim

By the time the second tower fell the Humanities lounge had filled up with staff and professors and students. I stood there and stared into the dust on TV. I was suddenly conscious that I'd spent years coaxing what I saw and heard, charting it as it traveled oxbow routes thru me. The dust disappeared the building. As I went thru the doorway, Bill said, "It's gone." I left the lounge and walked cross campus, the upstate sky unbroken blue. Kids on the library steps weeping in groups. I'd had a recurring dream where the students and faculty of the college paraded between classes holding their brains in glass jars, suspended in clear fluid. My thought then, "I guess neither approach is much good." Jackson Garden is back behind the Campus Center. I walk thru the stone gates feeling the towers and the dust and the broken glass of bodies pulse in my arms and legs where I'd coaxed the world to go. I see Thanha Nguyen, an exchange fellow in Modern Languages. When we met she'd told me that she grew up in Hanoi during the American War.

Last Spring, we read *Dien Cai Dau* in my seminar. I'd invited Ms. Nguyen to attend the class. I bought her a copy of the book and got Yusef to sign it for her. Her English wasn't great. She said it was hard for her to read in English when she missed her children like she did. I asked. A boy and a girl, 9 and 13. She read the book and came to class. She didn't say much. She turned to the poem "Tunnels" and told us that her school had been moved to a village outside Hanoi because of the bombings and that, for the first term, the teachers had worked with the students to dig tunnels like the ones in the poem. They were told to hide in the tunnels when they heard the sirens from the city. She said, after a few weeks, the tunnels filled with water and rats lived in them and none of the students would go in. Instead, they stood there around the opening to the tunnel listening to the sirens wishing the rain would stop. That's what she said. And, she turned to the poem "Prisoners" and asked if this writer was for or against the war. She asked why he wanted to bow to the enemy. I explained that the book's not really about enemies. It's about kinds of power and how they interact. Military, cultural, ancestral, erotic, psychological, masculine, feminine. I could tell she wasn't really listening. I pictured her standing in the rain. I stopped. She said, why did he want to bow to the enemy?

By the time I entered the garden I'd concluded that only a real fool would coax this fucking world into his body like I have. Naïve. My legs feel like they were sketched in pencil and then, mistaken, worked over with a wide eraser. I walk up to Ms. Nguyen and say hello. I can't decide if the burnt rubber smell is from the city or the scatter of tiny, hot twirls of the eraser burning my legs. She's staring into flowerbeds that bristle and hum with bees in the perfect sun. She : how are *you?* I ask if she'd heard. Heard? I say terrorists attacked New York City. Terrible. Could be ten thousand dead. No one knows. Ms. Nguyen's eyes turn to mine, she hands me her camera, "Would you take my photo with these flowers?"

1.

All American Erotica : A .38 Slug
in My Vocal Chords and the One That Got Away

You say I wear a sleepy-eyed mask

on my back. There were two shots, one clean

out the front; one a slow burn in my open
throat. We've come

a long way, learned to arrive
at airports early, the easiest shirt to wear,
the quickest story.

At home, tonight, the blinds
cut the light, the amber bottle in your hand.

You're in the corner of my eye, proof that it's not
enough to live

thru long odds. A coastline of perfume

sidewinds its way off your chest

and blooms its fist in the air above my head

ii

Once, we pushed up
to a bar and you said when you blink,
   you see me

   dead before we met. I watch you blink
watch the surface of the world
   close   *the surface close*

over me. You brush past and out the doorway
   and I catch a moment's flood

   of hallway light, and pause

   while the pool of skin-sloped scent

   becomes air. It leaves the shape
of Istria,

   my index finger finds Pula

   but it's already a crescent moon, windplay

on a pond, then Thailand, Chile, the S-curve,
   northbound

   lane, South Shore Drive.
The scent between us sheds its skin,
   its song floods the basement

   of my eye. I see it swirl up

   the heel-scuffed steps. You blink and it takes the light

iii

Every glimpse of you is a gift, flesh-flash

in deathchance that blew itself

out. Straight thru me. This scent
  from your breast

    stalks itself thru the long odds
of my body. I'm alive. You

blink and I die. Blind tip. Your tongue can't see
  the hard-domed

entry wound high on my shoulder.

  The one below, you say, looks
like it's sleep
  with a half-open eye. One

bullet's still inside me. Dead metal
  in my voice. You say that   *dead metal*

    when I say it,

  you hold the metal in your name

like the bullet's in your mouth, too heavy for its size

iv

You blink and draw back
like you've heard a two-by-four crack.
　You say, for you,

　　it's a red-light boy with his hood up　　*die bitch*
you saw the kick push back his sleeve.

His gun, jammed, is always there. Deaf click of an open O
　in your eye. You blink again, slow and long,

　　always　and I stay dead

　for ten seconds. Eyes closed,

you say the imagination's infinite, the chance

　　of meeting there unthinkable.
I'm wounded in a way that makes me think
　　I can heal

around the metal. You say no matter how
　much heavier than its size

　　allows,
it's not enough. No
　　matter the metal, it's no more than the sound

　　of sunlight and the taste of tin caught

　　in a bright sheet of water thrown across the grass from a pail

v

Like the shape of a scent, a voice with a bullet
  in its chords will never

    cover its shadow like lace

    thrown over the top of a mirror. As far

      as the mirrors go, you're right.
You hold one. I, the other,
  and light blows pieces

      of us thru the room. I watch you kiss
the mask on my back. You wink a glow in a stainless

      eye and scent shadows splay across the wall.
You're in your full-length robe
    of precision

and falling glass. I'm gone in blue light
  thru a broken window

    in your back, my limbs
break the beam
    into spectrums of useless motion. The exit route

took a piece of my third rib, you
  find the bone notch

    with a finger and say this wound's our fifth
nipple. It points away, rises   *always*
    to reach where the heat of your voice comes from

vi

The snare rhythm of Method
and Mary from a passing car,   —*foryourbodyandyourskintone*
   the wrong vowel's a pain net,

    a stress in a word can turn flock of knives.

    I gauze your face with my hands

    and every night we lost   *what we lost*

while you blink pours its wing-footed weight
   back over us.

    Eyes open, I see you seeing
me here. You blink. Pigments collapse
   into a wound

and lighten the skin around it. An orbit

    of surf against an atoll the weight of your name

   what we

lost   in my voice. The sound of that car rounds
   the corner, loops the block,

   you're all, I need—lie

   together cry together—they're police, you say, they love that song

I push you back, away
from the light into velvet shadows
    of the vestibule.

Clouded liquids
    from a bowed sky bent like real trust

        move between our mouths.

    There's always this

always between us. This metallic click. Our bodies
    open and pressed against

        the cold steel
of the front door, the El train's tremor, blue

        flash, suspends us

    over deaths, we wonder how, were not our own.

Flight 577 : Atlanta to Chicago : Seat 27 F

—after Raheem DeVaughn

In 27 D the woman beside me on AirTran
tells her year-old son in 27 E
   you wanna see daddy

don't touch that again   A six-week-old
   daughter in her arm

      a cresent-shaped scar

   on her throat appears thru frayed-end braids

she's dipped in peroxide
   Over the scar

      a sleek-eyed tattoo with angular brows
Under what the eyes know   in
   cursive

      about where the tattooed eyes' mouth

would be and diagonal across the scar's the word   *future*
   I'm helping with the boy's belt

      with one hand

   and trying my damnedest to get a no-look

photo of the tatt with my phone
  We taxi : the boy's got one

    earphone in his ear   the other in his mouth
she asks me could I turn

    the channel

  to "Urban Blast" and make sure he doesn't touch the control

ii

    —by the time we've got ourselves
up above the seatbelt sign
  he's out

and the earphone escapes his open mouth
  the baby's out too and the woman

    closes her eyes
deep   The future of what her throat knows

    stares at me thru the braids and she nods to the music

  her whole body nods baby's sleep

her head doesn't move
  My right ear's in the engine   my left knows

    the song :
suspended sentence   pain handed down
  that's the sound goes round

    and round

  —my brother's in the ground

bad-handed shuffle and a blank deck of fears
  eye to eye with a falsetto sky

    —women standing around   *broken*

    together and staring back at you like a jury   of your mirrors

Waking Up in Chicago after Dream Song 29

—for Jordan

    just short of a month ago I burned a first edition
on the hearth
    and scooped the blistered ash don't ask

into an airtight container I keep it next to the sugar

    sun up I stir a teaspoon of this shade and heavy cream
into coffee and there's breath clean
    as knife-wind in the brain blown down

the full length of the lake whipped into white waves

    they break on broken concrete slabs ice ripples
its hook-fingered rebar
    spine reinforced pearls condense

in the tight and curled-down sky parts of me

    in the hair of his forearm the lake's black & pitched on us
in sheets that catch the flame of the city
    in the air as for air there's just enough

for now the doors of the car frozen shut and it's him it's not him it's

    the taste of his voice in my mouth it's not my mouth
we talk every day which is never today
    til there's nothing to say til no ache polices his veins

til nothing ever ached like my mouth which is not my mouth

    for his as for now as if it was now and so ever would
the battery's *been* dead   quiet storm gone
  and we're tangled around each other for warmth

the past's nothing if not the irregular pulse of his lap

    in my ear and that cop saunters and wags
and pisses on the car and *thank christ* leaves us to freeze
  before we can't breathe   or just breathe

before we can't freeze   either way it was all there and now it's not

    go ahead : take the dice and let them kick up on the curb
you can walk away before they're still
  if you want but don't tell me there's no number

on the ground   don't say the last breath can't be the last

    and after that it's not breath   just don't ok
til you've kicked the rear window out & let night be this night
  and splash to life all on your face which is this face

that sounds that sound that sounds like that sound

like my hands that ache beneath this ice   as for friends and this ice
and love and Berryman : two out of three   (so pick three)
   will tell you what to do with rebar and wind in your mouth

and buildings that fall like needles thru your eyes : get

   the frozen flame in your belly and hipbones
cross to the wrong side of the rail gone raw and wave goodbye
   to what sounds that sound

and yes every weekend Ric's grandmamma Ms. Lou

   handed us her keys to Chicago and told us : remember baby,
every *good-*bye ain't gone   so you look   it's not like I haven't
   I've shut my eye and dreamed thru

keyholes and I'll be damned if she ain't gone on and gone missing

   too

Furlough Blues Sketchpad and My Abortive Stab at a Second Career in Interrogation and a Third at What I Get for Asking

I put it to bubbleboy and he popped,
left a perfect semiswirl of razormist where invisible
    sun used to be. I put same to circleboy,

    you guessed it, snap addict,

    flat line. I approached Suci while she memorized

the Presidents. Both pointer fingers up,
    eyes closed, she said wait, I love this

        one, Millard Fillmore. I'll admit if put on the spot
I don't always know if the past

        tense of swing is swung or swang
but I know I don't mean
    either one. I mean cause it won't go away.

    I feel dizzy when I think

a pendulum in orbit is always plumb.

I dissolve when I ask Mzée anything
    because he doesn't know

        where I begin or end. He looks up at me
from the floor, da da ca po—

When put to, chlorine spill pled triflouride
    and moved toward me

        in such a way that said, you don't want to know.
Said, you don't even want to breathe.
    I'll say I don't know if the past

tense of put is pat or pit. But I know perfectly
   well that there's no past

      tense of put. When I pit or patted it to whole add sugar

      packet of Kool-Aid in the mouth girl, she spilled

out a mile of something too bright to be
   looked at. Smiled. Gum line a blaze-coast.

      I knew better than to ask Milan anyway,
cause he can feel everything

ready to shift, and so I know he'll lie
   which isn't a lie so much

as a prediction of and against the impossible
   odds. If I pit it

      to him and he did, I know I'd tell him he lied
when I know I'd have told Suci something
   different if the same had happened

      between us. Before I got my lips together and breath
back of that for the first part of *p*

      Stacey turned around and told me (she may

      have told me then turned around)

      in no uncertain terms albeit wordlessly
she was "too busy with the present
   tense of her hips and *The History of Soul Train*

on PBS"—so you know what month it is—said
  "half the stuff in your head at any moment

    for instance" and back still (or again) to me touches her right

    index finger one by one to the tips of each

of her four left hand fingers and a thumb
  "unions, real schools, and us, and"—waving at the room—"this

    and"—waving at the kids—"them" and starting over
on the tips of her left-hand fingers "and February
  and did I say us

are probably illegal in the state of Georgia
  with or without *The History of Soul*

    Train on PBS and that pistol in the transcendental
drawer that *is* legal but I can't exactly say that
  can I about most of what I feel

like doing when I hold it in my hand" and my vision went
  all sketchpad and I saw how you draw hips

    and I saw circleboy
go mad and spin and spin and spin until he raised
  up and spanned himself back 3D

into bubbleboy who looked down looked me down dead in the eye

Verbatim II

If I turn my right arm up, on the inside beneath the bicep you'll find
the upside down smile Keith's older cousin Damon cut into it in 1979.
Faded, but it's there. Like Keith, Damon lived with their grandparents.
Damon worked nights at the Oscar Mayer plant in Madison, Wisconsin.
He said he boned hams. Damon always spoke low, it sounded to me like
he was speaking to a person too hopelessly far away to talk to anyway
and so what's the point. He left the house in his pea-green Impala at
nine dressed in what looked like a suit of fresh butcher paper. But, here's
the thing. He had cable radio in his room. *All* the Chicago stations.
And, he had a neat row of glossy Stacey Adams wing tips in his closet.
When he was safely gone, Keith and I would sneak into his room to
listen to his radio, the needle in the dial of his stereo glowed the perfect,
pale orange in Alicia Myers's voice, "I know it couldn't have happened
without You," singing the far-off color of the Chicago night sky.

We'd lay on our backs on Damon's bed. We tried to dance with his leather-soled, oversized shoes on our feet. Skyy's "Here's my number and a dime." We'd be on our bellies and squirm slowly against the bed and wonder what that feeling was. GCI and BMX moved in our veins and, when the DJ would say it, I could feel the thick slow jam spread all on my face. The song said, "Tell me," said, "Listen to my heart beat." Falsetto summers. Heaven. That is, as long as no one knew we'd been in there. Damon was evil. Keith's grandmama said so, said he'd been taken by the Devil. Way she said his name, like she was sucking on a hot pickle straight from Jew Town, we damn near believed her. She'd half say half hiss it, shake her finger at us, and spit-hiss the rest of some "you bet not be" phrase thru puckered lips at the floor in front of our feet. Keith's granddaddy seemed to agree, but we didn't exactly know because none of us could understand what he said. He talked without opening his mouth : sesu-mussu-e-say-say, hum. He talked without moving his lips : mesu-hey, hum? We'd nod. Yes? Ses, weum? Yes, Grandaddy? A language with its eyes shut. Words came out like sand you try to hold in your fist. Whatever he said, if we agreed, he was usually good for a dollar each and a twitch of his head that seemed to say get the hell out of his wife's house.

Damon *was* evil. I had proof. One night, he trapped us against the railing on the front porch, flicked his chrome lighter and rolled his hand slowly in the flame. Palm down, we watched from above, the bright twist glowed red thru bones in his thin hand. His long nails with clear polish. He parted his fingers, twisted his wrist, and let the flame spill thru. Said : thing about fire—and when he said fire it rhymed with high—you don't *get* burned if you know how to move.

Keith's Grand Ps slept like stones you throw in the lake and wonder what kind of forever they sink into. And, of course, Damon came home early one night to find us asleep on his bed with all his shoes thrown out in the floor. I woke up when the door to the room locked. There he stood. Radio on. Raydio. Keith's out. Wouldn't wake up til Damon slapped him hard and sat us on his bed next to each other. Eyes ablaze. He asked where we wanted it and he didn't sound so far off anymore. We figured he was going to punch us so we pointed to our shoulders. He : take off yourn shirts. He took out his flick-lock pocketknife and said he was going to teach us to be in his room and I thought he meant not to be in his room. Who wants it first? The glow from the radio was dark green on his face and revealed deep trenches around his mouth. Cigarette lit below his chin. One eye closed against the smoke, his other one on us made me think of when I'd hooked a fish thru its eyeball. The song, "You're the only one I love, and you can't. change. that." Damon took out the lighter and moved the knife blade in the flame til it smoked and the edge turned black. He wiped a smudge and its twin on his white sleeve and Keith told the floor he'd go first and I said that's fine with me.

Damon squeezed my arm in his hand and cut me first. Slow. A short, shallow, upside-down arc appeared in blood on my arm and I didn't bleed much and didn't feel anything except warmth that spread across my lap. I told Keith it don't hurt at all don't hurt at all. Keith's was almost a smile. I sat there in my soaked underwear and thanked Damon over and over and, somehow, I meant it. I don't remember thanking anyone and meaning it as much as that and I don't know why I needed to thank him and mean it like that but I can still feel how much I meant it same as I can squeeze my arm, now, like Damon did and turn it up and smile down at the frown. And, I can see his face and stare again at the wingtips toppled all over the floor. I thanked him and Damon said : never mind all that, just do whatever you got to do. Keith, in a voice I'd never heard before, asked the floor, why? Damon : cause if I ever see you in here again, or if anyone sees those cuts, I'll *go* to jail. I'll go to jail for cutting you'se little niggers' throats.

2.

Written in Oakland, Written Down

—July 8, 2010

In steel in open steam. In perfect
circles of this morning's
  comb-heist.

In your bathroom,
  in the tile's grid on my back,

   in what's left
of your heatprint dyed into strings

   lifted from lost rooms

  of my throat. Cold. Where night hides its slit

   face at daybreak.

In the fluted need of no one

person depending. In the bonecoat
  and staircase spine

   of a cruel thing that whispers
when lovers touch

   themselves thru the cell curtain.

  In each pore of the split trench

and skinmoat between us. In roomshift in blearwind

ii

Last night, when you crouched above me
  in the hallway. In light from the street

  gone red, shadows
of giant planets pulse your arms.

  I said I got here

  by tinfoil and waxtwist, bright

  threads in your hair.
In clockdrop in braintwirl.

  You said you always hear music.

  Said your body's a long curve that moves

inside itself. Up under me.
  Said don't worry about how

smooth all this is. It ain't nothing but a little

  skinpain. Just skinpain, baby. Code name

  for what nobody hears

  if they can't give up on doombright on deathspace
between long enough,

  enough to listen with their hands

  —*for Oscar Grant*

36

Bright Blindness   October 8, 1871 :   A Chant

*Chicago is in ruins, our supply of paper is cut off and we shall be obliged to
issue a small sheet this week without our advertisements. Our readers will
pardon us, and our patrons generally will favor us, under the circumstances.*
   —Marinette and Peshtigo Eagle, *October 14, 1871*

       no food where I was or much of anything else
there were whole settlements of people
      preserved by unknown odds

blinded by the heat of the night before   bodies everywhere
   in every possible state

       others in states impossible

       twisted around iron posts   placed clean

of flesh in unburnt trees   bleach-face down
   on black stones in disappeared streams

      heard about this from the sighted   a few
hours after dawn   found a road and stood there
   waiting   waiting   afloat

in the gone roar all around   nothing all around
      Dillard   a man my father knows   told me "had known"

       puts me in his ox cart   pulled me

to the junction   I stayed with the burying party until my sight come back so heard about it afterward   before I saw

any remains   built dark

   frames for pictures behind my eyes
from what I heard the men say and from what
  the women didn't   and from what

   I heard the men not say and from what
the women whispered to each other   built it
  for my eyes from what

I heard between the hard slink of shovels

   and raw clack of planks of pine

from the smell of soft coffins made from boards

   lifted out of half-burnt barns   and what I heard
was everything   not everything said   no   didn't listen

   to half of that   but frozen as they talked about the charred situation of bodies   piles of neighbors locked

around each other   burnt structures   I remembered

"look here   they knew enough to lock the animals
   out of the barn   then they ran back

      into the house themselves"   and I could see
time collapse and cry out in the voice
   of an accordion   humans

driven back before the fork in their guts   back to before
   they wasn't animals no more   the suicidal

      the animal impulse to seek safety
in man-made structures   I remembered how

      those wings of flame stole the sky from the night

could see them swim air washed out of the paper-thin

human skin   their brains knew better   freed the horses
   even chickens   then panic   ran inside the house

      for cover   I remembered the words

thru a thick smoke-filled beard : "we'll never

get them apart   like hiding from heat next to the roast inside the oven"

iv

three days   eyes stared into a blank white paste
   I watched my mind build the picture

    I remembered no color in the picture

    too bright for color   I'd always thought of blindness

     as a kind of deep darkness   mine was a flat
bright blast of unbroken white
    just about when I'd get a pattern built

     think I was getting to know how it was

    the next scene we came upon destroyed all what

sight I'd built   no use   the other thing always
   happens   then the thing other to the other

    and on   flame wings flew that night   high points death
traps   fire in cursive flesh   exile of air
    every high point bare black

with my eyes   that night   saw the fire move underground
   thru Carson's field next to ours

    we sat in the dark glow and roar all around

    we felt the house gasp   air stolen   the low whistle drawn

     thru cracks in the floor

v

    flame burst open in the high crown
of pines a hundred at once
  we heard a muffled sizzle and turned steam jets

from a line underground where the stream appears
  each spring the fire burnt under us even

    burnt stumps from beneath smoked

  like factory stacks glowed at the root *flare and dim*

flare and dim and when they dimmed a plume
  of white smoke from the top of the black

    stump the fire took its breath thru the stumps

    big old maple stumps from the sugar bush

  looked like the tip off

one of old Ogden's cigars thought out loud so much for low ground

vi

truth was   we found plenty of food
underground   wherever we went   a steady supply

of baked potatoes   turnips   carrots   rutabagas
    not much in the way of taste   skin burnt

        on the outside   but *wherever* we were   it was impossible

    to know   landmarks swept off   we knew

we weren't going to starve   not so for others
    down in sugar bush   four cabins

        in midst of a mile-wide swath of waste and hot ash
eight survived the night in a clearing
    we came across a young mother orphaned

of her newborn   she feeding the others   most thrice
    her age   most burnt beyond

        where she   blind for four days   could tell who
they'd been   who they'd become   who they'd been

        in the world before the wing burnt

    her baby to dust in her arms leaving her untouched   leaving her untouchable

her narrow breasts feeding bad milk

to seven blind adults   then six   five   until we arrived
   three days later   she   blind   feeding

   the two eldest   who   blind   held out

their ruined hands

that seemed to go to ash by the hour   she   feeding

   and we walked without sound on a bed of ash
leaf ash   ash of bone and sod   a soft sweep

   of ankle-deep ash   drifted in a breeze

long as a sightless three days   I felt the weightless

   weight of heat
in my own hands   a cow bell melted solid as the sun on silent brass

"Out" : June 11, 2011 2:24 a.m.–A Translation in Approaching Sonnets

Don't play it back to me legworn.

  Play it liptorn.

  Lay it out,
bodyshorn.

  And don't stop light
don't stop down
the heatplace, exact, coldspace
latitude of your arm.

  Move all what you know you damned do
along my face, move it til I see
what I taste.

  Lean back.

  Push yourself open
to fleshcatch, to an empty window of breath

ii

You be twenty-four hours in spherical air.

      I'll be magnetic.

      Clock-spun backward.

      You my, be fingers.

      I'll be sky caught in the smile
behind your knee.

      Ask who poured these
bodies over us?

      Spin like
the if in smoke; I'll be the color
of iron lost in steel.

      Continuous rail.

      How, you tell me,
am I not one minus three?

You be electric, hands all sprung
vowels & Byard, my mouth come to life

                    in your hair

iii

You dance your screen door, busted hinge.

    The sheer sky's black dress falls
on my face when I reach my hand
above my head.

    Me wrong as white
knuckle-splash
& a fifth slid out, arpeggio.

    After we spoke, I walked the vacant stones
of Omišalj, a high moon shone.

    I'm humming Byard bless the child when
a tiny mother scorpion
crossed my path.

    Her young, her back precise
as this liquid night, her body,
a hollow shore of time, darkpulse cast in un-filigreed light.

    —After Jaki Byard's "God Bless the Child / Lover Man"

Call It in the Air

        Last time I saw you on your feet,
we climbed Mt. Shavano
    to have lunch on the angel's hip.

Year by year step by step you lead me up
    past the line where trees grow past the line

        where shrubs cling to rocks

    and you tell south by the lichen. I hesitate

when my lungs begin to ache, lose a full step
    for your every two. We pass the line

        where grizzlies plunder pinecone stores

    of black, cat-eared alpine squirrels.

        Empty craters that smell of thin green air.
We're into the zone of the all too recently disturbed
    stones where grizzlies find moths

that blow in off the plains of Kansas
    and Nebraska to mate

        in the rubble beyond the tree line.
I don't want to know any of this, but I do.

        You do too but could give a damn.

    I'm scared and I can't breathe. I join the invisible

crowd of all those you've left behind and turn
   back and you're bears be damned

      on all fours now. I sit on a boulder and gasp
for air and I see you get smaller and smaller

and with each blink I see it flash clear.
   You could care about the altitude of the glacier

      angel up the slope. I remember how you used to
tell me I made you safe because
   when kidnappers came

they'd take me. The youngest. The boy. Now
   I'm bigger than you are, so,

      here I am, back here in the bell of the curve, Kate,
bait. And there you are,

      your liver floating in the numbbright,

   curled up like a peach pit

on a hissing radiator, eyes alight
   with the flamedarktorch in each pulse.

      I'm high enough
that my vision is splotched with black
   patches of torn cloth

and there you go, a slow drip of Patrón

and a quick whiff of nicotine

for lunch as you search your way alone out along
   the flat forever in the asymptotic line,

     search your way up for the line
up beyond which elevation

     the lungs change into birds
up high enough and cross the line to where

     you can go on living without having to have a body at all.

     —for Kate

And, But And : Decaying Sonnets

)   This weight of vanished leaf.
Or.
  Or, eyelash parenthetical.

Chin tangent to forehead. This incline
  of heat. Travel

    plans. A solution for inertia

leaned up on elbows, downward

glance in a bead of sweat. Runs your throat.
  Or. Or, wet

    crystal. Heavy light drawn
along a gliss
  of skin

    over rib shape, hipbone. Wind if

by land. Two if flies

    sprung like a mad wheel. Or. Or, quick.

Sketch the burnt span, a long taste of Spain.

ii

    You feign metaphysics & I'm there
with the *Adi Granth.*
  Skinware to open palm,

the GPS bleems in the route,
  the highway a sine curve flexed in salt

    down a frayed hamstring.

  Or. Or, text

    it.

Thumb it to me. The keyhole's open.

    The bridge

  is out. We can wait.

iii

I've got a handful of weapons. Or. Or,
   eye driven.

    Against riot thought
and Xanax. Let's push them from mouth

to mouth, spit the seeds aside
   until help arrives.

    Or. Or, plant. One

   in each hand. Or. Or, shade? Charcoal stroke

    and soft plunge of cosmos between us.
Or. Or, hand-sight.
   I've got this

gloss-built craft. Or. Or, torso.
   Spinnaker-bent

    against your next, your upturned breath   (

Freeze

I ask.

When they turn around I take my giant steps.

The ones I asked for. My dad works on the city.
   Road crew.

   I don't know why I'm scared
when tires hit gravel
   but I know my blood tastes

like if I put a penny in my mouth. Eyes closed.
   I wait for scratches on my face.

   I love the awful way

the word "whisker" pictures how

   a storm darks sky and does big
trees in the park. My dad's breath

smells like when the world goes away,
   like when I hide in the green

   fog behind "Old Abe," I put paper over the word
& rubbed it with my dirty thumb : *Continental.*

My dad warms it up. That means he leaves

   it alone. I love the spooky way
running in the rain

streaks my dusty face to where I look like my own
ghost, or something sneaky, an egg stealer,
   one that stays up all night.

   Before it begins, I can smell cold rain

   deep in my mom's hair where my fingers feel

the bumps start they start like when rain starts.
   In my bed, alone. I hear

   the house breathe. I love the only way
a summer wind blows night's long dress

   down our empty street. In thru my open
window, a shadow

   of a smile I can't see into crosses over my face

Verbatim III

West Bengal. India. Have an ear-taste. Kolkata. What a word lens to
objects? This is not a typo. I mean hold a word's lens to things. Front
seat of the cab. Let the meter run. Turn your face into the wind coming
thru the window of the car. Take a deep visible breath. Count the
inhaled parts. Ok, start over. Wreathed in flowers. Ganesh rides on the
dash. He's not saying. Up ahead is a flatbed truck. You're certain there
are physical pieces of it in your mouth. Upon acceleration, a slight
grade, whole tires come out of the exhaust. Your lips taste like the green
flaking off the rear bumper. The camera flails along, always too late,
capturing things just after they become what they're not. The endless
pattern. Revolutions. An abandoned pair of thongs on the sidewalk, all
movement in orbit about the empty space above them.

Was that bumper you said? And what are they used for in Kolkata?
More for tasting than for bumping. And driving? More for the exercise
in polyrhythm than for traveling. The driver's thumbs Morse an endless
code on the car's horn. Left thumb holds down the key. The driver
swerves right into oncoming traffic made mostly of bus grills, passes
one car, merges back into an eighteen-inch space. Right thumb takes
over the code. Someone's thumb answers. Several answer it, several
more them, etc. It's an ocean. The horns are fluid, audible everywhere
in the city. Your cab now occupies exactly an itself's-worth of space thru
which, a horn-thumb's second ago, you couldn't have passed your arm.
The accordion that, well, accords the behavior of this space is invisible.
It's an inaudible double, a moving mirror to the sound of horns,
the fundamental reality in Kolkata : motion inside motion and the
motion inside that and so on until the horns orbit the all-horn point, a
limitlessly small core of sound. And the mirror of that sound. A sound
point containing all the horns you hear, all the horns that have ever
blown, will blow. A point small enough that what orbits it moves not at
all. A mirror of sound silent enough that you hear nothing else.

Motion. A scooter passes with an impeccably lime sari'd woman seated sidesaddle, the pillion made of either a burnt-orange rag or the glow from the blinkers. You taste the oil stain in the towel's fringe and the blend of lime and orange moves like sunshine in an ice cube. The brushed steel bends your eye along a handlebar to the grip. The scooter pilot gecko-necks his wrist, his arm a capital *P* on its back, and the woman's hair tied back into an elegant knot of poise. Perspective bent. Chignon. Your right eye shouts as the scooter rides directly into the red grill of an oncoming bus, your left hears nothing and sees it emerge out of the back.

Let your eyes burn a bit. Keep your mouth open. Lean into it. The air burns your throat. Tears tears. Vision in your eyes like soot smoke on the thread-glass muscle of homonyms. Words and / as phrases for the layered galaxy of horns, of orbits : dorsalhoned, cacophelonious, infralogical. The horns sound the ruined beauty of a bazillion tons of bad stucco. Under their clothes, the horns wear the swish-pat of thong sandals on the sidewalk. An old man at his rig winches juice from cane with one hand, reaches into a parked car and works its horn with his other. A small mountain of smashed terra-cotta pots the size of shot glasses leans into traffic from the gutter. One slice of silence scrapes your cheek like lightning. For a splayed-open moment hanging in a butcher window, Kolkata is totally silent. You can imagine a way to hold the flanks apart and enter the flesh *Y* of silence. And, it's gone; you're the stem. A tiny boy plants his bare feet on the curb and waits. He's heard it as well. Which is to say he didn't. He blinks again, once, hard, to no effect.

Horns signal coherence. Signal chaos. The nuance and nerve-twitch cosmos of a living market. It feels everything. You can feel it feeling you. Street kids read something just a horn's rhythm to the left or right of your mind. They take shortcuts and appear between you and anything you turn toward. They know the market reigns. Work is time sold twice, stolen back, and sold again while the clock sweeps underneath it all in reverse. A barber works the traffic jam. Straight razor, dry foam on a pallet, he shaves the driver of a neighboring car who watches in his rearview mirror. The driver's thumbs don't pause on the horn as if the rhythm preserves his craned, taut-skin neck and the claim on the space his car and barber occupy. The space bought by the horn is the barber's overhead. In your mouth, you taste the flat brass of a moment come alive. Presence. Sold. Night doesn't trade in flesh for nothing and it doesn't wait for the day to end. It passes in a rickshaw, bright sky rolled up and tied with a sash, it opens east down a mother's red sleeve and glows on the bridge of her son's nose. The Baul play the night's raw silk for whatever's on your mind to give away. The music's thumb on the pulse of light's own way of agreeing to disagree with the dark.

3.

Basso Ostinato

Memento, homo, quia pulvis es
—Cristóbal de Morales

And the split chrome of a bent fender
meant world   said move
said baby needs you   leave Vienna

in your lost ear   in bright flake over black
rust   stealth drones test what's over our heads

Keith Jarrett streams the morning

pushing his blind spot

across the stage   each line a scar
on this page   world : baby   go   baby

need   across fault

lines we inherit from the tabletop

the pedal says   low
says lower   down to what you've got   :
sustain   :   wait : you forgot

to make it rain   was it god
or law said : that woman bleeds you   if not

who   or was it all inaudible
sound   a simple nod   we've each learned to do

—she says in birth   what hurts the most
 is the body getting itself ready

   to push : repeat : push

   delete   after that it's what rhythm knows   rhymes

colors in a newfound chord   what lord
  could live with what it does   with its tongue

     between your toes   & some of this or most
within a coil of what we make   some get

cake fingers play riverain ache as dusk draws the coast

iii

An eyeline at most   physics says you can
   put your head against a stone

   all day   & no work done   a baby
tooth buried in a slice of apple

      finger on a bump of bloodline in the gum
my father knew if he was at the job
      he got paid to work   walked the floor to check

joints at lunch   checked the torch
   at coffee   he'd taunt me   point at stacked pallets

      of brick   "30,000 over there   you'll touch every one
three times"   I asked him once

about the men who worked for the union : organize
   he said   like his father said about his

      uncle   organize? they work for the union

   cause they don't *want* to work   told Duffy

at the job I think—and he cut me
   off : ain't nobody   ever   gone to pay *you* to think

—someone you'll never know tunes
   out "Imma Be" to visualize the probable glitch

      in an Arc Scan circuit   turns off Evening
Creek Drive   digits on the dash : Z-90.3
   steers in silence over pristine asphalt on electric

power   parks the Prius in B-12   steps
   into a high glove of Mylyn dusk

      blinks into the stereoscope   palm open on the screen

      swipes the ID card   vacuum lock

opens and closes   blue light and a pulse
   of negative ions voids the cube of air

      walks ahead under two signs : the first :
GAAS, INC. LEADING THE SITUATIONAL AWARENESS REVOLUTION
   before the next lock and arrows :

      ↑ ROOM 21A SAR—SYNTHETIC APERTURE RADAR
   →ROOM 22B GMTI—GROUND MOVING TARGET INDICATOR

the second sign : ENTERING DUST-FREE ENVIRONMENTS

v

If I buried all this and you dug it up
you'd know I think my father wondered why
  all life couldn't be a job

the sacred pressure of industrial history   of versus
    of the law of one at a time testing each pulse   of work

    in the heart of labor   something
you didn't have to love

    to scowl at   at one lunch break

I stayed out of sight   pulse in
    each raw hand like holding my own

twin hearts   & listened to myself listen to the men talk down

About their wives   my father   back turned   on his knees
    running hands over the smooth tar

        covered slab   seven a.m. it'd be wet
with the night's sweat   a sheet of black glass

        first thing was to dry it with the torch

        without heating the tar   first thing was to wave

the flame over what you're afraid to think
    you are   the men talk & I don't

        know I'm listening til I'm ready
to hear what I want not to want to hear   and I didn't
    look but I can still wear a mirror

of his sneer on this
    union scale face   and my father's going to say something

        and he doesn't know I'm listening
and I know how men talk   and he : my wife?
    wouldn't take a million dollars

        for her   wouldn't give you a nickel

    for another one   quick as that

        he's back nose to it   making sure
that dusty black-slipped piece of concrete
    stays as flat as he's going to tell the boss it'll be tomorrow

One day, my big tiny fearless terrified sister
laid on her back & showed me
   that death is the slowest breath   now I know

   four ways to count to four & I know any baby born wants

more   some days I still feel like she'll come around

   the corner thru my door   my finger on this
key like a bald head against a stone   the pilot fell

   asleep and that plane overflown   asked Stacey what color was

that woman's tooth in Faulkner? And, she : roan, baby, roan!

The day I sprinkled ash on your hips & the day
you pushed and pushed & we didn't
  want to know vows scar the body & didn't

  want to know out into what?
& didn't want to know how vows breathe
  thru rain-on-tin in the book vows

  the body took how neither of us see my ear
swallow your arm what car keys do
  all night on the hook a pulse thru teeth

  in closed water of the mouth the reef
sound of coral in an upturned wrist a.m. sun holds it
  down and we circle a bright stack of pages

  on the wood there's a sworn-to twin
of this divorce in city hall
  I know a vow hard as corner iron

  in your eye the judge with his fucking drawl
far as this state goes we were never much
  here et al. and marriage the right

  to look away heavy vows
rattle rivets in the freight
  vows hover but we know drones don't

  float we know bridges never cover
what bridges uncover in the moat when we lie down
  lover to lover two other bodies roam a ten-eyed level house

ix

By anhydrobiosis   (life sans water)   the microscopic
  twin-twirl-headed bdelloid rotifer

    avoids being taken by fungus   it gives up
all water   becomes nothing

    to eat and lighter than any movement
in the air   a scattered cloud
  of dust   avoids predators by avoiding

nothing   as nothing   by being
  as close to everything

    as something that close to nothing can be

x

Quick as the flick of capstan to wippen
notes run the slow-grown grain of spruce,
   song of sun in the room when your father told me

what your grandfather told him
  (and so what he's telling me) about his daughter

  and what he didn't know

  your uncle Will already said

about his baby sister's baby girl on our wedding day :
  "Congrats & welcome to the family, son,

   I meant what I said on that microphone,

  and I mean this : good luck, you know she's got people

   and you're never alone

  and I know how it gets and if it gets bad don't beat her bring her home"

xi

The cut felt voice of a low chord strike   tap

and knuckle hold up the damper   Prototype

drones arc "delocalized" air as a baby
   fights sleep with what's inside

   his fist   none know exactly why
the best hammers are made

      of pear   but he knows night is time come alive   how
what's all around come inside us in the dark

      knows by what touches touch and taught me
   to press but don't push into

   a push that don't press and he'll slip away
into sleep   Jarrett plays again
   and its slice of itself by Sébastien Erard

   invisible mechanism of repetition   you go
and your scent banks

      away from him   I read today "domination is a rhythm

   we move within"   I hear the shower I can
smell sweet steam get deep   it's 9:15
   all the things I know   in no light

and don't   what a Predator's pulse will and won't
   in both my hands   dark wings   open on this

baby's back   here   and let all shadowslip in the eye beyond that

Soul Music and Firearms and the Blue Light on My Stoop That's S'posed to Cool Motherfuckers Out but Maybe It Doesn't Work

Sit here dipped in the sound of ice
   in a glass in the sound

      of the rubber

   fringe of the fridge door   Sit here

and wait for the song
   to repeat and repeat and take me

      apart   here and wait
and apart and wait for the phone

      not to ring and not

to ring and not and when it rings

it's the Georgia State Patrol wondering
   if they   *this can't be*

      what they said   can it?

can come on over and finish the job

      Sit with these drum-machine ass limbs
and hair-trigger brows
   set

at locked and loaded   Bet your woman's
   other man's bottom dollar

      on these hollow fingertips

The neighbor from the crack spot next

to the church   *c.m.e. you think I'm lying?*   hips

his dips past the house he doesn't nod or turn
    he knows better

        than to question the bass line
pulling the night's breath
    from under

    my door or the slow curve   *glow*

        of red on the back of the blinds
The red?   That's just me

        and the hell of me and my old friend Chicago
and the stripes

    on my hands   The glow?   We're at it again

    listening to Deveon

on the only YouTube hit we could find for Smoke
    City   My friend's last

        name?   Cutlery   You should see the metal
tusk smile
    at me close-up in the red

and the glow

and the hourglass of memory

in Deveon's lost voice   My friend here smiles
  a missing eye

    tooth and Deveon blows and I turn
around as if he's in the backseat
  of Big Ric's Porsche and he's not

    Deveon's last name?   Overton : And Big Ric's Porsche
no saying where he got it but I'll say this : you could leave it unlocked
  anywhere on the South Side

and come back and find it gone until you find it
  back washed   waxed   and a new joint in the ashtray

    Now here in this broke down Southern town   tonight
the name of the one now he's dipping his hip

    back past the house?   Don't know
From the doorway I say "Going

and coming"   And he "you know it"
  as if
                    asif

    he knows I know he knows something
And as if he hides most

of himself and whatever he thinks
I know
  he knows behind

the white-hot crack curtain laced
  in his head under his brain

    like a mirror-blind

  pillow He's the lucky one

Least that's what he insisted last night
  when he stopped

    for a light and cocked his pistol *a .38*
looked like to me
  and pointed it

at Luna and Lucy slow-dragging with

  the stoplight pole on the corner of North and King

63rd Street Station and / or
a Quiz : Pronounce the Word Spelled : C l o s e

You stand above the platform
and an apparition of Ezra
  Pound

whispers, "get back now" when she says you don't
  know the dangers of skin

    ribbons and how they can

    knot when you let an ocean swim

thru you. She said you can't see the knots.
  Can't

    touch these ribbons. This salt won't stick
to the rim of the glass and won't gather
  up the backs of your lips.

    Said, left
to themselves, most dangers are easy, they burn clean

    brass in your mouth. Oceans cello

    hair-thin veins, freeze silent wires in your throat.

This is not a word

    we're allowed or the past tense of shut : c l o s e d

ii

C l o s e. Say it. Careful. She says she won't say it
because it's a trick. You, said or not
 it's a fact. C l o s e d.

   It's not quite the same as open and it'll peel

  you into skin ribbons, take your legs,

a silk hem turns scythe blade in the reeds. Close,

   close.
In this way we're mispronounced. Closed.
  Your knee gives

   and straightens as she walks away
and you think there's no word for—

   Well, when you hear all kinds of things that can't be said.

iii

A candlelit table in the window across

the street, Atlantic Starr sings "closer

than most." The song's tongue curls
and plays the concave brass backs
    of your teeth.

You think about the living
    weight and all the roar all around this train,

    an invisible

falcon wears a satin mask. A green bottle

    waved over dust
on the olive.
    You tell yourself it's impossible

not to walk away. This request doesn't exist
    in our language :

    please, close me. Neither this

warning : careful, you can't see this

is what your hands do when you hold them over your ears.

iv

Ever felt a hand open on your back
in a silent way
    like when a tide decides it's gone

out and begins to come back in? And you knew it
    wasn't your hand and you knew it

    wasn't the hand of anyone you know

and you knew it

was why one strings a wire over a death yawn
    and you knew it

    was the lost skin of wind from what
ancient sails were made.
    You've been

    close. Ever dive under a volume,
a thunder-white swirl of fingers that crash

    a too-narrow cove? You've been closer.

Tried to wink underwater and found both

    eyes tied to your wrists tied
to oak posts

    in a moonless room? You've been closed.

Closed : the uncertain condition

of being close. As in

what's always unsaid in the saying : open and closed.

v

We know we've got ten fingers

for eighty-eight keys.

There are things we can and can't do.
   The tortoise proved it

      to the hare and the worm
begged it
   from the bird.

But things move inside other things, too.
   Closed. Overhead, right now,

      a fig proves it to a bat and we are here

and there's still no word for what or where we are.

Give and Go Gave and Gone

In work boots and woolen Wigwams, you better
cherish the day and act like you know
    we're a cold wind in summer trees at

Sligo Park. After all
    the shins crossed up in Gainesville,

        Bridget can be anybody

    she can have off the dribble. Give

Tiny the ball in the cage and there's nothing
    he won't do

        if sunlight slips between strangers.
Shut Up and Play filled lanes in the flesh weave
    at Nat Cole Park when L-No

fell in broken glass on the wing and you knew
    you had Jone Jone trailing by sweat

        beads in his used-to-be-*your*-woman's
perfume. She was here

she was here yesterday, sat off in the grass
    like Sade sounds in the shade. Sweat.

        Damned if something something just ain't right

    about how we do each other wrong.

        If you pass it to Ranger,
don't *come* around tomorrow. The only place

in town I know your pulse

before your name. If you see Shame, tell him we waited.
   Remember the day we won three

   straight? The sunset, your palm on fire, come down
in the chain net and never swore a sound

   until Red and Ricky opened a trunk full

   of joy and rain. You know me, I'll whisper it to you
and go right. Two bounce : *you know why loving you is easy?*

   Slap the board on a crip— *cause you're beautiful.*

One death-still midnight in June,

   we met alone under the streetlight spot
at center court. I asked about that heavy
   hand

and you said Rough Shape was out there in the parking lot.
   On Saturday, you showed up

   with That Scratch, our shadows slow danced
in the lane and I tasted salt

   from the smooth brown dome raised up on your neck.

Who else can tell them? About Maurice

   at James Madison and the blood type of my shirt when I put
point in his eye. Last night, you wore my skin home

   and it couldn't have meant less if I liked your punk ass.

It's a Dream Wherein Finally–and by that I mean right away, which is to say, just in time–I Understand Circular Breathing

it's my first class in the infra-tactile studies program it meets in the
Incunabula Collection of the Bancroft

it's Nate Mackey's class
    Professor Mackey is young

        wears jeans and Professor Mackey wears a brown leather belt

    a big, oval silver buckle with inlaid blossoms

        the heels of his black cowboy boots worn round on the bottom
I dream turquoise
    I know it's a dream

        I don't turquoise
I think I really think the perfectly edited reel of twists

think wow black boots brown belt
    I don't know how I know it's Berkeley but in the dream I know it is

        don't see any of the other students but I can smell dark coffee

    elsewhere the taste of sunlight a strobe in my throat

        and it's as if Nabokov's father is being thrown up in green air outside
the window and there's a cat there and I know it's there
    forever to lick dust from blue miles

    of silk
though I don't see any and I don't remember anything else about the room
    but what could be called polyphony if polyphony

        meant density and if density
meant the touch-profile of coffee elsewhere if elsewhere

meant somehow
the satin texture of a bright strobe in my throat
   Professor Mackey stands there leans elbows on a stack of books, laughing,

beautifully, as if laughing was a way to learn
   to fold discrepant creases

      into invisible paracritical cloth

   and I think laughing even if it's a kind of thought

      ironing in a dream
just can't be done any better than that
   Professor Mackey wears a black T-shirt with a red

neckband (and in my dreambrainsomehow it's a "r-e-a-d" neckband)
   I know none of those books he leans on are written

      in language and the T-shirt

      has white block letters on the front that read (and in my

somehowdreambrain they "r-e-e-d") : TRANSCENDENCE IS *SEA*-LAVERY.

Verbatim IV

Why carry these heavy veins of nightfall? Why let ribs swell with
pleasure of swimming metal seas littered with ankle bones and misplaced
situations? Tendons and temptations. If your upturned face leaves a stain
of sweat on the sheet, and I say you've stolen back all the lefthanded
pores and rhythmblooms locked in my empty chest. You say, try English!
I say, you can't deny we've both steadied ourselves on the path with
sandstorms of thought coming thru the soles of our feet. You : speak for
yourself. I say I talk to hold your eye, a still pool in my hand. The bald
arrow of breath on an open wound. I've followed the run in silk up the
back of your thigh, traced the riff-ridge of invisible hair along the edge
of your tongue. You : I'll give you that, for now. But, don't think of
leaving it there.

There was the dream of the war over faces. Scalps left intact. Fields of the faceless dead. Cheekbones chipped. Music of hollowed skin. Scalpel squadrons. The run on apple corers at Family Dollar. An alphabet of blades into hitches behind the ears of the fallen. The black market of features. Runway models stalked the cameras wearing the final thrust and brittle creek of a soldier's brow, the lip-shorn intensity of a battle-mouth. You : watch this, I'll nod my head. You : this explains that. Me : this? You :

http://www.youtube.com/watch?v=SmhP1RgbrrY

Me : that? You :

http://www.nytimes.com/2007/07/08/books/review/Murakami-t.html

Me : right : this *is* that : Monk : "It can't be any new note. When you look at the keyboard, all the notes are there already. But if you mean a note enough, it will sound different. You got to pick the notes you really mean." Look back at this. Swept leather sole of the rhythm. The white face of the smooth floor. Technique part anthology of drum-stroke, part to summon the harpist. And, Monk's right hand above the keys, the hover, a mantis in its own faux wind. And, Beckett's problem : how end? Brush the crumbs, the ones you mean, from the table. You : and the ones you don't? Me : the knife is two knives stuck in the same board.

Remember this when you're two-finger-walking your way thru my records. The impulse is to hunt *this,* us, down. Hand me that would you please? To hunt this down. Put me down. The impulse is to rub the dry reed beneath her eye. That'd be you. You : would it? The impulse is to listen again and again. To drip wax in my ear. The impulse is extraction. To examine the fluted mold. Listen to Lester Young resist the impulse to give in to brass. Listen to him choose wood. Tone more breath and spit than whatever note. How much does the scale weigh? "Without Your Love." Lady's voice a razor of skin tone in a bottomless cloud. Brass refused again. That invisible trumpet she held at her side. The whole note there on the first count, the rest a pulling back. A touch-siphon, prism in torchlight, veins held in the ripe center of a pearl. There's not a single word in this song. English is an alias. An alibi. Lester Young plays "I'm Confessin'." The terror of both arms gone. Of vanished hands above his elbow. Beyond the wrists, a mirror inlaid in the octave key. Gloss on chrome made of metal refused, made of wood held open.

4.

Visiting Hours at the Color Line

These Stateville phones won't speak the words.
The night we slept together

    in your cold furnace
of a project bedroom. Place so full of faces,
    we drew circles around each

    other. Love. Anger

thick as smoke from James Sr.'s chalk-faced

    wife.
Her white sons down
    the hall. Their metal gong in the air.

    Your older brothers? *I'm rolling thunder,*
fire and rain. When it comes
    to evil,

    I'm a hurricane. Sugarbear
in diapers with sand hair and ash legs.
    Pre-Desert Storm Anthony

    still had legs and ran low and
studied his French in a green

    haze. Still sent us on dollar-a-joint runs
to 301 Building
    B. This glass is bullet

    proof.
You toss your head : "the white witch
    of the north."

We don't talk about that first
frozen night on fire
   with Sugarbear's baby blanket. A smoke ring

curls in the empty air, I see her
   lip-line draw up and I didn't want to hear it

      cock-suckers   then and I don't want to remember it now

You really didn't hear her did you?
The radiator spits
   stars out the broken window. Chicago's

   got us stuck between

its teeth. We don't talk about how I woke up

but you never did. Chicago's
   kicked-in smile. A stainless hall

   and a series of open wounds clang shut.
Your bed concave with the nude
   heap of books

   you found
out in the trash bin. The nickel
   scent-shadow of a burnt

.38. A single sheet skin-stained the color
   of where funk comes from.

   Here I am in front of you now.
This pin says I'm visiting. They say you're here
   for life. Your laugh

   hasn't changed. You

tell me how the slumped-down man in the next

booth got his. You stare at me loud
  enough for him to hear

    you blink. You don't. The glass. Crushed
:   *don't.*   *glass.*
    starlight in a chrome mirror

iii

You do James Sr.'s Blue Bland on the plastic

couch : "I know you've been hurt,

by someone else. I can tell
   by the way, you carry yourself." Eyes cocked

   and waved down the metal hall
at his wife's white sons,

   "I'll take care of you." Your smile's unchanged, man.
I breathe it all back into the phone

and it sounds to me
   like "smiles unchain the man." We don't talk

   about that. Instead, the old drunk you heard
whisper at us. You : "had him his
   last nigger that night"—I nod. "tried to hide in a phone

   booth?"— Again. Your eyes drill

the glass, "believe that shit?"—And, again

iv

    A streetlight hails down at frozen buckles
in the salt-stained asphalt. I see the first
   brick,

mine, smash the glass.
   The second hangs in the air with your name

    written down its rough edge.
He's still calling us

    names. And you. Again. Again. Again.

   Until he signs   *signs*

the sidewalk and steam leads   *leads*
   the way up from what's left

   left
of his mouth and what's left
   of his mouth looks to me like pieces   *pieces*

    of three mouths. I'm running right

   now. Now the blasted booth

    of his helium voice running thru the sound
of ice in the streetlight's reign of color
   broken all over the ground.

His legs twitch, electrified Ss in your eyes.
  Here. Our lives carry us

    on their backs and we act
like we never knew the difference
    between the

threat of liquid in the wisp and we fluid froze in the whisper

We shut your room door, Glen Jones's voice
   from speakers hung in a green net

at the ceiling drowns the head-banging

    down the hall. "Show Me." You say this music makes

you quiet when you hear a door open
   and a bad man's voice

     starts telling you to kill. I nod but my head won't move.
I hear a lake
   swallowed by an empty moon. You

say your white brothers are cold, no matter what,
   a stone tastes dry in your mouth. You

    say Sugarbear's what love

smells like, but he's only half your brother. You

say Anthony's the real one and he's got drawer full of wide
   open black girls and a big thick book

    full of different ways to kill everyone
he knows. Chicago. Any pock-mark
   eye's part ricochet. Chicago.

    The light goes out.

  The city sings.

    You ask if I can see the falsetto dragon caught in the net

vi

Sleep swings over a charcoal mouth, elevator reek

and empty shaft. Awake or not, I hear Luther :

"a chair is still a chair." Low
clouds gather and lie down over me
    and tight hairs on the wet heat

of your thighs scratch my ears. Elements
    in the room come apart. Cirrus-blue ice. Rain on burnt

    slate. My body's a pocketful of loose change
dropped on the tabletop. I'm 13.

Hairless. I have no hands. My arms end in a grist-ghost
    above the false ceiling of your skin. As

if black ice could swallow

    the night's white sky of flame, there's a shadow

    of a sword in my throat

and a pearly bloom wipes my brain clean

Ink Bells ring. Guards. Closed wounds
in the hallway come
    alive again. You smile   *smile*

and stand to go, hands slack-chained to steel rings
    at your waist : your eyes swing back to me, "don't forget

the times I saved your life." I nod.

    And the window goes dark. Again. I'm blind. Again.
My tongue's extinct. A bleach-clean
    wing bone.

    I can taste you

    thru the glass, the first gut-stroke of body heat,

the rank vein and sudden silk

    of your pulse   *pulse*   your pulse on my breath.

Ornette Coleman's Out-of-Office Reply

This? It's bone crystal. New growth.

It's a full-fluted pain bristle. No

mistaking the hand-hewn Gullet of It All.
  Note the rhythm. A brand new

    dimple in bare flesh within a stun gun's easy
range of ivory tickled

    in the shadowed side of the room.
Here, keep it. Watch it, wash
  away.

Heavy minerals remain. Let high mountain air

    drink the blue and leave salt rivers

on the sun-brown back of Dr. Fear's

unstudied understudy. Watch out. It sees in the dark.
  Ms. Curiosity Killed It.

    You can almost feel it all
happen. Can almost hear the chrome eye
  of the engine wink

    your name. Me? I'm the keeper.

    Curator, really. By now you must know the routine.
The perfume and the smell of glue

on an empty

gum line, the stone's throw from noonday

to nowhere. You've pad-prowled
   your fair share

      of throat-garbled nights, called their dream-stolen
names. You've tasted dust from legs opened
      and tangled into treble

clefs, hands gauzed to stem the bass hum.

      You've gone back to check

      the slipknots. Herr Sleight-of-Hand, rag in mouth

and tied to the posts. Doused the bed and tossed
   the match.

      Behind barn door number three : the Deputy
Provost of Insinuation
      cuffed to the nickel catch

beneath the sink. If it's still you on the line, leave

      me a message, lover. This isn't news
if you've cupped red

      hands and blown our secrets into pools of rain

that freeze by morning into nerves

    of steel.
You've slung vendettas back at false
    ceilings and cursed the clean

shaven sky. Chin flung up

    and veins chalked beneath the skin,
you were there

    when I told the sun to go back down,

    dared the moon to try it

    with its own broke-down luck in the lost and found.
Or don't.
    Sit there quiet and work

    that loose flap of skin, the one that, admit it,

    you can't bring yourself to leave alone,

that trap door in the floor and the balloon-eyed bottom
    feeder hanging by its tail

    in the smokehouse. Let's don't mention
the broken picture
    window you carry around

in your pockets. Go ahead, hold back

and let the easy gait wear the legs raw. Or not.
It's up to you. Dig in for chaos
　and exact change

　　for the bus. Here it comes. Dig deep and make
no mention, the red
　　river

of knuckles down your leg. No one will notice.
　Put your lips up

　　to my absent ear and tongue-touch me

a stolen prayer. It's not music, it's the hollow howl,
　frenzy of the invisible

　　stain, the blood-curse of songbirds
gone extinct and gone down

　　a slope slippery as the green

　stretched thin

on crooked old Mssr. Nothing From Nothing's false eye teeth.

From : Arachnida Speak

we too carry dreaded glands in our abdomens
they hold secretions from our dark ages
   born in true flame

honed in flat-toned howls
   sure-footed dances

      we bear the chemicals of our struggle

   some feel them useless

burdens in the face of this nimbus gnarl
   this plenty

      sudden varicies become seizures of remembrance

   how eyelashes turned centipedes in your sleep

sentinels stalked your face
   our own mythic bugaboos   hair drew back and rattled

      noses and talons grew sharp

   arms feathered

of course we had patterns of our own then
   premonitions   gifts of shadow

      nook and boon of darkness

   our metabolic pact with rock and hard places

ii

so now you know it's coming   again
unfathomed still

taken in by appearances   carousels   rotisseries of
  plumb believers

    baked in booths of still light and peppered

  with the haste of relishers

rivaled only by the Pentium whirr and quadrazillioned crackle
  of avarice

    you've dug in well pilgrim
amazed as were our enemies   we'd thought
  the plains' wind

would blow you all away   we watched you
  tear at your ears for generations

    now the howl's distant   a red Doppler glow

  barely stirs leaves in the street

    after the storm a sunrise lifts

    the scent of a daughter's hair tangled in a field of wheat

something in you too   cousin   feared our enemies
  we owe it all to you now

    our golden age   we breed colonies

in what you've fooled your fool selves into knowing

cutting-edge vassals
  we were prepared to wait

    but in your heady leapfrog with evolution
in scant centuries
  you've murdered most of our foes

and with your telescopes in orbit can almost see
  the dragonfly

    never mind the solution for gravity

beheld   our web in four dimensions   Forms

hallowed and pristine   crystalline lens and cast-iron mask
  belief stalked and mothered

    by fear   and time   have you any time at all?
if you'd only pause

    we'd gift you our sacred jewel of night

    we'd let you have Chicago and time enough to die

Alibis for the Heavy Part of Rain
That Stays in the Sky

I've got no every   when   tongue
or other   where   design.
  I could lie and say you were always on.

  Bench bluebent toward a hollow sky.
One right next to mine.
  Face pull weather thru reinforced glass.

  Wouldn't say why.

  Born like that sunspots run

  your tongue; now
he's a slipslice of eyenight to pass.

  Could say, last life, you were always right,
there, strummed lost names
  on your borrowed guitar. Might say he was heavy

  as thread-thin air;

  I could say you still are.

  Or claim barefoot. Shoes full of shells
peeled off pistachio stones.
  His shadow bowed bright, road wound

  down in dust-splashed light—

  your Uncle Will kissed a melon on its skin

  like his sister's cheek,
called it a letter from home.

  Why not? You're all right.   Right?

How about ran-over, worn leather,

 floptongue suede on the frozen
concrete? Brass rivets, hand-hammered.

 Truth about this?

 Some spit-shine defeat.

 Skip the feather, the day we got old, silk
band on your hat. I'll say safety
 blade thin call him Three Month's Rent.

 You know where all that's at.

Call it what you want, too, stick around

 or get back. Way I see it
it's up to you, count on me. That'll be that.

 And you'll know it sure as Gimme got shot
and too legit to teach to sit.

 Or not.
And, either way, sure as anything
 you forgot, it's up my back,

 round my neck no need to check,

 the image has been spit.

 I'll say you'll know him when you don't,
see him? I don't have to say sh—never mind
 think.

What's the matter your mothers never
taught you all to blink?
   Call yourselves, what? Pass him in an empty street.

   He's got my some of my stompedallon

my swallowedandgone; hidden off

   in the tall weeds of the slow need case the lights come on

      —*for Mzée*

✧
✧
✧
✧
✧

Verbatim V : You Two Talk or In Flew Itity : Epilogue

SCENE

A park bench faces the house, a breakwater at the edge of the stage, cityscape behind

Man One sits. He wears a suit, tie, fedora, and overcoat. Bottle in a bag on the ground

Man Two approaches. He wears a suit and raincoat. No hat. He sits on the bench next to Man One

It's 2:35 a.m.

Man Two speaks first (Man Two speaks—or doesn't—in the top of each couplet)

Been here long?

What you want to fight, too?

No. Why? How long is what I asked?

Why not? They all want to fight.

Well, not me.

Yeah, right. I know, you're *different.* I've been up all night.

[under breath, looking away] Just my luck. [turning toward Man One] Looking?

Yes.

For?

A new way to come out and just say it.

Of?

Good choice. I can't answer that. The point.

Say what? And, out to?

No, it. And, if I can't answer "of?" then—

Of course. Of course, understand, when I said "luck" I meant merely—

[cutting Man Two short] Got a light?

Matter of fact. [handing Man One a silver lighter] Demonstrable. Can you say how long you've been looking?

[pronounced after a pause, slowly, while slowly taking the lighter from Man Two] We'll see about that. Very nice. [holds the lighter up to his nose] I love the perfect blue smell of butane. Like a brushed steel sky, just before dawn.

. . .

I'm not sure if I'm looking.

But, you said—

No you said.

But you said—

I know I said. Yes.

And, I said "looking."

Yes.

And you said "yes."

Yes.

And, so.

[places the lighter in his coat pocket] You see now you're looking. But, now that you're looking, that does seem like what I've been looking at.

At what?

No, that.

. . .

Ok, I know, make it plain. At what you said, "for a new way to come out," and so on . . .

You said that.

That's what I mean. You said "looking?"

And, you said, "for a new way to come out and just say it."

Yes, there! You see, you said it.

But, not until . . . [leaning back as if to get his first good look at Man One] Have you really been up all night?

Yes.

Here? At the lake?

Yes.

This lake? Have you come out?

Yes. No. Have you ever seen a star set?

A what?

A star set.

You mean a constellation?

No, no, no, no, no.

. . .

[motioning down with his index finger] A star. Set.

A falling star?

No. A setting star. Have you seen a star set?

. . .

You can't see it move. But, damned if you can't see *that* it moves. Train
the eye. Try not to blink. The color deepens. Don't think! The object
lowers but you don't see the color deepen or the object lower.

. . .

Stars move thru a spectrum when they set, they turn a low red when they meet the horizon. Red so low til it's nearly, nearly blue—

[Man Two points out over the house] Show me.

Can't. Far too white . . .

What did you say?

I said, too much light. We'd have to be too far from here and [throwing up his hands toward the city in back of them] then there's all that all over us . . .

Do they enlarge? I mean when they set. Stars.

There's no way to tell. But they turn red. And, it can't be denied, [intensely] you think you're staring at *it* move, but you only see *that*. [fists raised to the horizon, teeth clenched] While it moves, never. the. less. It moves on. [calm defeat] Tell yourself whatever lie you want about it. While you see that. It moves on.

. . .

You see red. And it turns.

[looking at Man One, leaning back with a kind of concerned / intrigued smirk]

You look at *it* and see *that!*

And.

And something else happens.

What?

I don't know.

But, you know something else happens?

I do?

You just said it— Wait, oh, no I know . . . now I've said it, right?

You may have. I said I didn't know. I may have dozed off. Like my own
little bird-boned poppie used to say, [savoring the words] "resting my
eyes."

But, you said something else—

Look, do you know anyone you trust? I mean trust enough to admit that
you've said what they've said?

What does that mean?

Are you saying you don't know what I'm asking?

No. Just wondering why you ask?

Never mind. I've got my answer.

Do you?

Yes. I do. You trust no one.

I don't know if you've got an answer at all. Could you give me my lighter back?

Do you have to go?

I'd better.

Why?

You know too much.

[takes the lighter out, flicks it open] I know nothing.

That's way too much.

Which is to say? [pause] Have we met? [puts the lighter back in his pocket]

Which, if I follow you *this* far, like everything else, is to say something that probably shouldn't ever be said. Not that I'm aware of, no.

I'd say that far. It's hardly been as far as this . . . and, yes, you'd certainly better go. Demonstrably, so. That is, if all you want from this is that.

Do you swim?

Yes.

Did you swim last night?

Yes.

What's in that bottle?

Don't worry about it.

Is it yours?

Yes, always. Who else's can it be? In other words, who's else?

What's in there, your swimsuit?

[thumbs flick at his lapels] I'm wearing my swimsuit.

You swam last night?

Yes.

Wearing *that* suit!?

Wearing it still. In light of all this. In spite of all that.

All what? Tell me about it.

No, all this. I can't.

Why not?

There'd be no way to tell you about it or this and continue.

Continue to what?

[shakes his head, waves his hand to let it pass] To protect myself and [picking up the bottle] my considerable wares while . . .

While you tell me?

No. While I'm swimming. And, without a will without so much as a gentlemen's agreement? Without even so much as a, *rapprochment* . . . [takes a drink] Are you crazy? [tips the bottle toward Man Two] A sip of my private quintessence?

[waving the bottle away] Why would you go swimming?

To tell you, of course.

At the risk of sending you back in, are there lines around here? Lines lying about that I'm missing?

Lines?

Right. Demarcations. Possibly, lines of thought?

In the lake?

In or out. I don't know if it makes a difference.

To whom?

What? To us?

[incredulously] You want to know if there are lines of thought in the lake to us?

No, a difference to us. Not lines to us.

[removes the lighter and flicks it, watching the flame] Do you think we use our imaginations to turn ordinary acts of life into symbolic gestures? Some shabby impulse to permanence. To filmy myth. Something left, left of us. Leaning. I mean the constant thrusting back. In the mind. I mean in order to elude certain, bourgeois infectations in the absence of ideology?

Do you mean infections or, possibly, affectations?

[as admonishment] It can't be avoided, you know? I mean just what you said.

Which? When?

No, what.

Ok. Wait. You said "I mean just what you said" by which you meant you mean just what I said which, wait [wagging his finger]. Heh, heh, you're at it again?

No, that, actually. What you said. Inevitably.

You mean to say that you *mean* "bourgeois infectations?"

That's that. It's hard to mean be mean, as mean we mean to be. I might mean the failure of ideology, not the absence of ideology, now that I— I mean it failed, you know? It was destroyed and the soil it grew salted down. Now, people just out here trying to feel stuff— [slowly, with cut eyes] Cop a feel, you know— [making "feelies" with his fingers, both hands] Trying to avoid swimming.

[repeating Man One's "feelies"] You know, when you say swimming like you . . . [shaking it off] Ok. "Infectations" it is. Such as?

[staring off, a riff of whistling . . .] This is how I act. I mean, while I'm waiting.

For what?

[continues whistling] No, for it.

Swimming?

You might have said hot showers. Or, sex on perfectly clear, thin ice . . . over a winter stream in the mountains. It's like levitating! The fear's the best part of it. One feels the cold beneath one begin to fail. I say, it's levitation! But, we can go with *that* it if you like.

I hadn't thought of those.

I see, sir, you are a liar. [staccato] What else is there to think ay-bout? [legato] Much less think about talking about? Unless, that is, you're ready, which is to say you've got the *guts,* to tell me your failed ideology. [adagio, taunting] No one escaped, you know? And now all the mind's thrusting . . . all the copping and the feeling and—

[cutting him short] How about swimming, for instance?

Can't be done.

And, why not?

One either swims or one doesn't.

And thought?

Never, no. Not about swimming. Thought stops before that gets to swimming. To attempt to think—much less talk!—of swimming is to fail, to arrive at something mistaken for swimming and to think about that instead. In place. Of it. And, if one should attempt to talk about thinking about swimming, one talks about something even once more removed. We should just admit that. *All* that. The thatness.

How can that be?

Exactly the question! The fact remains, in thought leave aside talk, *that* is; swimming doesn't.

Doesn't what?

No, it. Be.

What if I go now, out in the lake and walk until I can't and then swim and think about swimming while I'm out there. [said in such a way as to subtly tantalize] Why, I bet I can swim, think about it, and *tell* you what I'm thinking while ["feelies"] swimming.

[as if he'd been expecting Man Two to say that for years] Well, yes. [pause] That's that that just all about it isn't that, so so common. That that's almost an era all to that's self. Is there no word, "thatself?" Should be. Were all it up to me, would be.

[mockingly] What is "so so common?"

That shell game you suggest. Thought hidden under the facedown cards of doing. Action. Romance. Is *that* really what you want to do? All to keep from doing any of it. Against it. For it. As *if* it, any of it, a flash-dash of it, a flight-past-light-herd-of-neutrinos-thru-a-trophy-raddish of *it,* matters. Matter. Is that why you always want to fight? It!?

I said I didn't want to fight. Truth is I can't do it.

Oh, I know, I know, I mistook you for the prototype. Truth is you can do it, but you have to think that.

No. Truth is—truth is I can't swim.

No doubt. But, that it doesn't matter.

Why?

Why because it doesn't exist.

[Man Two understands, as if to confirm this much] Ideally, you mean.

[leaning in close to Man One's ear, whispering, with obvious pleasure] Pre-cisely.

So, then, ideally, if I'm swimming and thinking about swimming . . . if I can't do that, then what *am* I doing?

Ideally, now?

Yes, ideally.

[distractedly, blowing on his fingernails, as if totally beside the point] Drowning.

Why do you say that? Ideally, it doesn't matter if I can swim.

That's exactly why I say, as you said, that—though I didn't say that. By what I said I meant *it*. Drowning.

I thought swimming was it?

[in wild disbelief] Sir!? [tapping his temple with index finger] Until you're think-ing. Then swimming becomes that and drowning becomes it. Can't you please follow me to this? I mean stroll with me. Down the winding lane to this. [said to provoke] That's where we're all headed you know. [chin up] Thisss. This is where you and I are headed. Right now.

But, why did you say it, that, whatever you just did say?

Say what? What you said?

Drowning.

Ah, there. You just said it, you see, often it has so little to do with far, far away that. But, you're absolutely right, of course. As you do well know as you know you well will do. [suspiciously, head up, as if asking the sky] So, why ask me why I said it? [turning to Man One] Are you being coy with me, sir? Why, I think you're flirting with me! [looking about and shifting closer on the bench, then in a whisper] My good man. Are you flirting with me?

Would you give me my lighter back?

[opens up his hand, looks down at the lighter] I most certainly will not. Let's float a little further. Can I say I'm glad you sat down here with your lighter? Your hatless self. You're not a fighter at all, are you?

No. Yes, you can.

May I?

You may.

So, let's count it as just said, then, shall we?

Float on.

I submit. An American must take a shower. When an American takes a shower, inside that one, somewhere, exists other people's touch. The imagination. [and then speaking slower and slower] Rivers run down, lighten the color of the skin. Order and disturb the thinnings and slightenings, the fine coverings of hairs on the body. [leaning toward Man Two, and slower] Order and disturb.

Well, there's a leap.

Not at all, rather a fact. A dynamic fact. The best kind. And, want to know the good part? It's the only kind. Get down next to a dynamic fact. Truth. You know, a piece of shrapnel. Get down next to one of those and you better hold on. It's windy. Turbulence in the very Earth upon which you stand near any fact in life.

But is it, I mean such a slowness in the speech, necessarily sexual?

Aren't all prayers?

Ok, how about no politics or religion. And, what about baths?

No danger of that at all. And, no, there's no reaching in a bath. None whatsoever.

Don't tell me, I know, baths can't be thought about either.

Don't be silly. Have you ever swum in a bath? Even ideally? It's got nothing to do with thought. Baths are body mirrors, sensual realities. The sea. Close relatives of the skull, the gourd. A grape. Flick a switch and watch the bulb go blind. Globe. Baths, my dear hatless non-combatant, are now! Showers are strangers, man. Rivers and alley tricks. Freeways. On their way or nothing at all. Never present tense. No presence sense. Never. Got it?

Um, ok. And so, swimming?

When prayers are answered.

I thought I said no—

The river means the sea. It and that. Then and now. The prayer is always again. Please, again. Again, please. The end of your little scabby little prohibitions : [scoffing] politics, religion.

So, swimming means—

Death.

And, drowning?

[factually] Can't be done. [sardonically] What you gone do, die twice?

But, haven't you just been swimming? At least ideally.

Yes, at least.

And?

I'm pausing dying just to talk to you— A vacation. After this, back to dying.

If I can't have my lighter back . . . And, I mean, since you're on vacation. Would you kiss me?

[in falsetto crescendo] Doubt it.

Why not?

Cause you'd tell everyone, as you always do, that *that* that was *it*. And, even more, that that so-called it, the it that that was was my idea. An invisible cobweb twisting, catching dust and so catching such does come to light. In sight. Like any flick-in-switch just might.

Why would I do that? It was my suggestion.

Uh. [to the house] There he goes again with his siddity infectations. [turning to Man Two] I don't mean the kissing, silly, I mean the swimming. What are you, paranoid?

[shaking head under his breath] Feels like drowning to me . . .

Always does always does never let there be a doubt . . . it's a good sign . . . all which in any case, liar, you said you couldn't do. And, so, here you are [pausing and looking around] on this bench, proposing I do for you what you can't do, or say you can't do, for yourself. [pause, slightly over-pronounced] Proto-Typ-ic-al.

[in defeat] Touché— Don't we all? I say it's the very least you could do. [resigned and slightly vindictive] I'll let you keep the lighter.

[slipping the lighter into his lapel pocket] What does the song say? "Stone that the builder refuse . . ."

I don't know it.

[Man One traces his index finger up Man Two's throat and off the bottom of his chin] ". . . touch that the swimmer reuse . . . kiss that the drowning abuse."

So, is that it?

[Man One stares at Man Two who looks away after five seconds]

[Man Two staring at the ground]

[Man One touches Man Two on the chin and turns his head to face him] It is never that. But, it can be ever-so-close, [leaning toward Man Two] maybe once in a while close enough, to *this*. And, *this* is, as you said, what I've been looking to do.

[a kiss . . .]   [curtain]

Notes

The epigraph by James Baldwin comes from his essay "Every Good-bye Ain't Gone," *New York*, December 19, 1977.

The epigraph by Henry Jackson comes from his catalogue *Henry Jackson: New Work, 2010*, available through Cain Schulte Gallery, San Francisco / Berlin.

The epigraph by Geraldine Hunt comes from her dance classic "Can't Fake the Feeling."

Acknowledgments

Thanks: to the great staff at The MacDowell Colony and to Nicholas Allen and Julie Dingus at the Willson Center for the Humanities at the University of Georgia for providing time and space in writing and revising the work; to Henry Jackson for his brilliant vision and for allowing me to use a detail of "26-10" on the cover; to Dan Beachy-Quick for selecting the manuscript and to Stephanie Stio for all her work at the National Poetry Series; to Ms. Jo Chapman at the Lannan Foundation, Ms. Lea Simonds at The Juliet Lea Hillman Simonds Foundation, Stephen Young at The Poetry Foundation, Mrs. Stephen Graham, and Mrs. Seward Johnson for their work with and support of The National Poetry Series; and, of course, to Daniel Slager, Allison Wigen, and the staff at Milkweed Editions for what they do every day.

Many thanks to editors and staff (and to editors who are the staff!) at magazines and anthologies where versions of these poems first appeared: *A Face to Meet the Faces: An Anthology of Contemporary Persona Poetry, Apocalypse Now: Poems and Prose from the End of Days, Ploughshares, Black Renaissance Noire, Chimurenga, Harvard Review, Red Wheelbarrow, Indiana Review, Inertia, Illuminations, Memorious, Ninth Letter, The Owls, MiPoesias, Urhalpool, The Cortland Review, Wood Works Press,* and *Open City.*

Ed Pavlić's most recent books are *But Here Are Small Clear Refractions* (Achebe Center, 2009; Kwani? Trust, 2013), *Winners Have Yet to Be Announced: A Song for Donny Hathaway* (University of Georgia Press, 2008), and *Labors Lost Left Unfinished* (UPNE, 2006). His other books are *Paraph of Bone & Other Kinds of Blue* (Copper Canyon Press, 2001) and *Crossroads Modernism: Descent and Emergence in African American Literary Culture* (University of Minnesota Press, 2002). His prizes include the National Poetry Series Open Competition, the Darwin Turner Memorial Award from *African American Review,* the *American Poetry Review* / Honickman First Book Prize, and the Author of the Year Award from The Georgia Writers Association. He has had fellowships at the Vermont Studio Center, The Bread Loaf Writers Conference, The MacDowell Colony, and the W.E.B. Du Bois Institute at Harvard University. He teaches at the University of Georgia and lives with Stacey, Milan, Sunčana, and Mzée in Athens, Georgia.

Interior design and typesetting by Allison Wigen
Typeset in Adobe Garamond Pro